About this Learning Guide

Shmoop Will Make You a Better Lover*
*of Literature, History, Poetry, Life...

Our lively learning guides are written by experts and educators who want to show your brain a good time. Shmoop writers come primarily from Ph.D. programs at top universities, including Stanford, Harvard, and UC Berkeley.

Want more Shmoop? We cover literature, poetry, bestsellers, music, US history, civics, biographies (and the list keeps growing). Drop by our website to see the latest.

www.shmoop.com

Table of Contents

Introduction

In a Nutshell

Euripides (480-406 B.C.) was a misunderstood genius. He is said to be the author of around 92 plays, but he only won the big theatrical competition at the festival Dionysus five times. His final win was for his undisputed classic, *The Bacchae*. Unfortunately, Euripides didn't get to enjoy this final triumph. Being dead kind of got in the way. His son ended up directing the play for his deceased father. To add insult to injury, Euripides died by being ripped apart by a pack of wild Macedonian dogs, or at least that's what some people say. It would be a pretty ironic ending for the playwright, considering all the dismembering and body ripping that goes on in *The Bacchae*, one of the last plays he wrote before he died. Some scholars say that this grisly story of his death is fictional. We hope they're right. Euripides deserved better.

Poor Euripides was always getting picked on. Aristophanes lampooned him mercilessly. The comic playwright made fun of Euripides's use of language and his characters' tendency to spout the new fangled philosophies of Socrates. Like his buddy Socrates, Euripides's ideas were hard for mainstream Athens to swallow. This was due in part to his progressive ideas. He was anti-war, sympathetic to slaves and women, and so critical of traditional religion that many believed him to be an atheist. Athens, while being in general much more "enlightened" than may places, just wasn't ready for these "liberal" ideas.

Euripides was known to be kind of a loner. He spent most of his time writing in a cave on the island of Salamis. Eventually the lack of appreciation for his work and his disgust with Athenian politics (especially the destructive Peloponnesian war) may well have been what drove Euripides to leave Athens. He spent the last months of his life in the court of the King of Macedonia, where he proved them all wrong by penning his undisputed classic, *The Bacchae*, and perhaps met a pack of dogs with a taste for playwrights.

In *Poetics* Aristotle rates Euripides as much lesser tragedian than Sophocles, pointing out Euripides's haphazard plots and un-heroic heroes. Sometimes these criticisms are true, but we wonder if Aristotle ever stopped to think that Euripides had another agenda all together. While his rival Sophocles was towing the traditional line, Euripides was busy inventing entirely new genres. In retrospect, we can see that it wasn't necessarily that Euripides didn't know how to write a traditional tragedy; he was just dissatisfied with the form altogether.

Euripides's loosely plotted plays with happy endings created the genre of romance. His focus on the emotional lives of his characters along with his comparatively natural sounding dialogue foreshadowed by thousands of years the creation of modern realism. By blending comic elements with tragic, Euripides basically created tragicomedy. In *The Bacchae*, for example there are all kinds of funny moments. We're pretty sure Pentheus prancing around in lady's clothes got a few chuckles, even though the audience would have been well aware that he was about to be ripped limb from limb by his own mother. This blending of the humorous and horrific was revolutionary.

When *The Bacchae* got its Athenian debut, we bet everybody way back in 405 B.C. was like, "Hey, why didn't we pay more attention to this guy?" Sophocles definitely gave Euripides some respect. In honor of his deceased rival, Sophocles dressed the Chorus of his own play in black. If there is a Hades, we hope Euripides can look up and see that history has vindicated him. More of his plays are extant (still around) than any other ancient Greek playwright. Euripides is now known as one of the greatest and most innovative playwrights to ever walk the Earth. We're glad the man has finally gotten his due – he was basically a one man dramatic revolution.

If you want to learn more about Euripides and his work, check out TheatreHistory.com.

Why Should I Care?

Have you ever had trouble letting loose? You should talk to Dionysus, the Greek god of wine and revelry. We wonder what songs Dionysus sings in the shower. Maybe he's into a little Beastie Boys – "You got to fight for your right to party!" Perhaps he's more into Kiss – "I wanna rock and roll all night and party every day!" We're positive he bobs his head to some Nelly every once in a while – "It's gettin' hot in here. So take off all your clothes." What we're trying to get across here is that this guy really likes to throw down. It's his job after all. Boy, does he do it well in *The Bacchae*. He inspires every single woman in Thebes to throw a big dance party in the woods.

Of course, the revelries that Dionysus inspires in *The Bacchae* are much different than your average party. Dionysus's followers don't just party for partying's sake. Their wild gatherings are sacred rituals. With the acceptance of Dionysus into their pantheon of gods, the Greeks recognized the importance of such events. They recognized that society must create an outlet for release. If we as humans don't build in time to let loose, to get a little crazy once in a while, all that control can build up in negative ways.

On other hand, the play also shows the dark side such festivities can create. Dionysus rituals get totally out of hand. The participants get so wrapped up in his wildness that horrible violence results. It seems to us that this struggle to find the balance between control and release is one that will never leave human society, making the play just as timely today as it was when it was first written.

Summary

Book Summary

At the top of the play, the god Dionysus prances out and tells us he's in disguise as the mortal form of the Stranger. He's come to Thebes to spread his religion. His wild rituals are a big deal all over Asia, but Thebes is the first place in Greece where he's brought them. The ruling family of Thebes, the house of Cadmus, has managed to really tick the god off, by denying his divinity.

Dionysus also fills us in on his whole life story. He's directly related to the main folks who are denying him. His mother, Semele, was part of Cadmus's family. She was also a lover of Zeus. That is, until she was tricked by Zeus's jealous wife, Hera, into asking Zeus to show her his true form. Semele's puny mortal frame couldn't take the king of the gods' super godliness and she was obliterated. Dionysus was still a fetus inside her when this happened. In order to protect his unborn son from Hera, Zeus stitched little Dionysus into his thigh until the child was ready to be born. Since Dionysus's birth, the rest of the royal family has denied that he's a god.

Dionysus is now determined to show them all. He's started by turning his mother's sisters into the Maenads. The basic job description for a Maenad includes: dancing in the woods, drinking wine, breast feeding baby animals, and dismembering whoever gets in their way. Dionysus summons the Chorus, a group of Asian female followers, to dance around the city and sing his glory, while he goes off to the mountains to frolic with the Maenads.

Cadmus, the founder of Thebes, and Tiresias, the famous seer, show up all decked out to worship Dionysus. The two old men are wise and know better than to trifle with a god. King Pentheus, Cadmus's grandson, storms on stage. He's incredibly mad about all the women dancing in the woods, especially since one of them is his own mother, Agave. He declares that he'll stop the spread of this new and terrible religion no matter what. Tiresias and Cadmus tell him he'll be sorry, but the stubborn Pentheus doesn't listen.

Pentheus's men bring in a chained Dionysus. Of course, they have no idea that they've got the actual god on their hands, since Dionysus is in mortal form. They think the Stranger is just the head of this new Dionysian cult. King Pentheus mocks the Stranger and tells him he looks girly. The King locks Dionysus up in jail, but swiftly regrets it. The god summons earthquakes and lightning, flattening his jail and ravaging the palace. A Herdsman toddles on and reports that the Maenads have gotten even crazier. The Herdsman and his buddies tried to take them into custody, and the women went nuts, ripping up cattle and raising hell all over the countryside.

King Pentheus determines that it's time to summon his soldiers and kill all the Maenads. However, Dionysus convinces Pentheus that he ought to go and observe the rituals before he makes his decision. The only way to do this, says Dionysus, is for the King to dress in women's clothing. Pentheus is dubious, but after the god places him in a weird trance, the King is all about cross-dressing. This works out terribly for Pentheus. Dionysus sells him out while he's spying on the Maenads. The ladies go into a frenzy when they see the King. Pentheus ends up being ripped apart by his own mother, Agave.

Agave returns to Thebes, bearing the head of her son. She's so deep in her Dionysian delirium that she thinks she's holding the head of a lion. Her father, Cadmus, knocks some sense into her, and Agave realizes the horrible thing she's done. In the end, Dionysus appears in all his godly glory. He curses Cadmus, saying that he'll be turned into a snake and must lead an army of barbarians in battles against Greece. Agave ends up being banished from Thebes. At the close of the play, the Chorus sings a song of praise for their victorious god, Dionysus.

Prologue

- The god Dionysus, son of Zeus, enters.

- He tells us that he's in disguise as a mortal.
- The god tells the audience about how he was struck from his mother, Semele, by a lightning bolt.
- He points out the remains of her house which still smolder and flicker with magic fire.
- This was all a trick of Hera's, who was jealous that her husband Zeus was having an affair with Semele.
- Dionysus praises his grandfather, Cadmus, who made a monument of the place his mother died.
- The god talks of how he's conquered places all over Asia, but Thebes is the first city in Greece where he's spread his wild rituals.
- He says that he's mad at the sisters of his mother, Semele. They spread a rumor around that he isn't really the son of Zeus, that his mother just slept around and after her death Cadmus made up the story.
- To pay Semele's sisters back for their insolence, Dionysus has incited them all to a frenzy. Currently, they're all dancing about in the mountains, and soon Dionysus will cause all the other women in Thebes to join them.
- Dionysus says that he's mad at Pentheus, the King of Thebes, who doesn't pay tribute to him as a god. The god tells the audience that he's going to teach the King and all of Thebes a lesson. If Thebes tries to resist, Dionysus will lead his followers in battle.
- Dionysus calls on the Chorus, female followers he's brought from Asia, to dance and sing around the city.
- The god goes off to the mountains to dance with the women of Thebes, now called the Maenads.
- As he makes his exit, the Chorus parades in.

Parados

- The Chorus sings of how they've abandoned Tmolus to follow Dionysus.
- They chant about how awesome Dionysus's wild dance parties are.
- The ladies talk about Dionysus' birth, how Hera tricked Semele into asking Zeus to appear in his godly form, lightning, which obliterated Dionysus's mother while he was still inside her. Somehow the unborn Dionysus survived the blast.
- To protect his son from Hera, Zeus sewed Dionysus into his own thigh, where the baby stayed until it was time for him to be born.
- The Chorus sings about how when Dionysus was first born he was swaddled in writhing snakes, and that's why his followers, the Maenads, twist snakes into their hair.
- The ladies beckon the people of Thebes to join the wild ritual dances going on in the mountains.

First Episode

- Tiresias, the old blind seer, enters.

- He's dressed in goat skins and ivy, which are the basic uniform for Dionysus's rituals.
- He bangs on the palace doors, calling for Cadmus to come join him in the mountains.
- Cadmus, Dionysus's human grandfather, enters and greets Tiresias warmly. They talk of how they're both really old, but not too old to boogie in the name of Dionysus.
- Pentheus, King of Thebes, enters.
- The King is super mad. He's come back from abroad, because he's heard that the women of Thebes are out partying in the name of Dionysus.
- Pentheus has heard that big old orgies are going down in the woods.
- He says he's arrested some of revelers and will soon catch the rest. He's even going to arrest his own mother Agave.
- The King blames all the trouble on the mysterious Stranger with golden hair who has charmed all the ladies. (Pentheus doesn't realize that this person is Dionysus in human form.)
- Pentheus says he's going to find the Stranger and cut off his head.
- He thinks the whole story of Dionysus' birth is a lie.
- The King notices Tiresias and Cadmus all decked out for the rituals. He criticizes them both, saying their old and foolish.
- The Chorus leader interjects and tells Pentheus that he should be more respectful.
- Tiresias chimes in as well. He tells Pentheus that Dionysus is indeed a great new god. He's brought the magic of wine to Greece, now the people have something to help ease their sorrows.
- Tiresias says that Dionysus will soon be one of the most powerful gods in Greece, and that Pentheus better recognize him.
- Cadmus warns the King, his grandson, not to trifle with Dionysus. For one, says Cadmus, it's nice to have a god in the family.
- He also reminds his grandson of Aceton, a man who got ripped apart by wild dogs for saying he was a better hunter than the goddess, Artemis.
- Pentheus is less than convinced.
- He orders that somebody go and trash Tiresias's house to teach him a lesson.
- The King also demands that someone capture this mysterious blonde Stranger, so that he can be stoned to death.
- Tiresias tells Pentheus that he's a fool and hobbles away with Cadmus to beg mercy of Dionysus.

First Choral Lyric

- The Chorus sings of how terrible Pentheus's blasphemy is.
- They point out that willful men like Pentheus often pay for their disrespect.
- The ladies sing of all the lovely and blessed places throughout Greece.

Second Episode

- A Soldier shows up with the mysterious Stranger (Dionysus) in chains.
- The Soldier tells Pentheus that the stranger didn't put up a fight at all when he captured him.
- There's also some bad news, says the Soldier. All the ladies who were arrested escaped. Their shackles magically fell off and the prison doors flew open.
- Pentheus comments on how beautiful Dionysus is, implying that he's too feminine.
- The King asks Dionysus where he's from.
- The god tells him that he's from a place called Lydia (a kingdom in modern day Turkey).
- Dionysus (who's still disguised as a mortal) says that he's been sent to Thebes by the god Dionysus.
- Pentheus asks if Thebes is the first place that the religion of Dionysus has been brought.
- The god replies that he's spread it all over Asia.
- The King says, that figures because Asians are stupid.
- Pentheus tells Dionysus that he's going to shave his golden hair and put him in jail.
- As Dionysus is taken off to the slammer, he tells the King that there will be vengeance for his actions.

Second Choral Lyric

- The Chorus pleads with Thebes to save itself by honoring Dionysus. They call on Dionysus to squash Pentheus's brashness.
- Suddenly, Dionysus' voice is heard.
- The palace is shaken by an earthquake and lightning.
- Dionysus appears.
- The god asks the Chorus if they were worried when he was arrested.
- They say yes, because they're lost without him.
- Dionysus tells his followers that it was easy for him to escape.
- He tells his followers that a spell was cast on Pentheus. When the King thought he was tying up Dionysus he was really tying up a bull.
- Then the god set the stable on fire and flattened it to the ground.
- After that, a phantom version of Dionysus appeared in courtyard. Pentheus chased the phantom around until he collapsed exhausted to the ground.

Third Episode

- Pentheus busts out of the palace.
- He sees Dionysus and demands to know how he escaped.
- Duh, says the god, I told you I would.
- Pentheus orders him recaptured and all the city's exits sealed.
- Dionysus comments that that would all be a real waste of time.

- A Herdsman enters.
- He tells the King that he's come down from Cithaeron, the mountain where the rituals are happening. The Herdsman asks Pentheus if he's going to punish him for saying things that he doesn't want to hear.
- The King tells him that he won't punish him for honesty.
- The Herdsman goes on and describes the rituals he's witnessed.
- He says he saw three groups of women lying on pine needles. One of the groups was headed by Pentheus' mother, Agave.
- They weren't all naked like Pentheus implied earlier, however some of them were breast feeding baby animals. (What!?)
- The women picked up staffs and struck the earth, making water and wine spout from the ground.
- The Herdsman says that he and his fellows tried to capture Agave, but when the Herdsman laid hands on Agave she cried out to her fellow Maenads. They all went crazy and ripped the Herdsman's cows apart with their bare hands.
- Understandably, the Herdsman and his buddies were freaked out and ran away.
- The Herdsman says he watched the Maenads raid the villages at the foot of the mountain. They snatched up babies and looted people's houses. Their heads were on fire, but it did not burn them.
- The villages through spears at them, but the attacks had no effect.
- After they were done with their raid, the crazy ladies went back to the fountains and washed away the blood. The snakes in their hair licked their faces clean of blood.
- The Herdsman tells the King that Dionysus must truly be a god for all of this to happen.
- He points out that the god's gift of wine to Greece was a great thing.
- The Chorus Leader tells the King that there is no greater god than Dionysus.
- Pentheus still isn't buying it.
- He orders all his soldiers to arm themselves to go and fight the Maenads.
- Dionysus tells him that's a really bad idea. The god offers to take the King to watch the rituals for himself.
- Pentheus is interested but suspicious.
- Dionysus tells the King that he'll have to dress like a woman. If the Maenads discover he's a man, they'll surely kill him. Pentheus agrees and goes off to find his best drag outfit.
- Dionysus announces that he's luring Pentheus to his death.
- He also says that Pentheus will be beguiled so that he'll walk through town in women's clothes, humiliating himself in front of his people.
- Dionysus says that soon Pentheus will be murdered by his own mother.

Third Choral Lyric

- The Chorus sings of a fawn escaping a hunter's net.
- They warn that men who disrespect the gods are punished.
- They sing beauty, joy, and punishing rivals.
- The ladies chant about how human hopes sometimes find success, but often come to

nothing.

- They finish by saying that the luckiest men are those who are happy day by day.

Fourth Episode

- Dionysus enters and orders Pentheus to emerge from the palace.
- The King enters, wearing women's clothing, a long wig, and dress.
- Dionysus has placed him under a spell.
- Pentheus says that Dionysus looks as if he has the horns of a bull (the King is seeing Dionysus in his god form now).
- The King starts acting all prissy and asks Dionysus if he looks pretty like his mother. Dionysus acts like his nurse maid, adjusting his dress and wig.
- Pentheus talks about how he'll hide in the pines to observe the Maenads.
- Dionysus tells the King that he will take him safely to the Maenads, but that another person will bring him back.
- Pentheus says it will be Agave, his mother, who will carry him back.
- Dionysus agrees, saying she'll carry him in a very particular way. (Insert: ominous music.)

Fourth Choral Lyric

- The Chorus sings a song of vengeance.
- They bid the hounds of hell to whip the Maenads into a frenzy, so that they will destroy Pentheus.
- Justice, they howl, must punish the sacrilegious man.
- The Chorus prays for Bacchus (Dionysus) to come as a bull, a many headed dragon, or a fire breathing lion to trap Pentheus.

Fifth Episode

- A Messenger bursts in. He announces that Pentheus is dead.
- Praise Bacchus, yells the Chorus Leader.
- The Messenger chastises the woman for celebrating such a disaster.
- He goes on to relate the horrible circumstances of Pentheus's death. (Warning: this is seriously messed up.)
- The Messenger had accompanied Pentheus and the mysterious Stranger to spy on the Maenads.
- The three of them hid in grove of pine trees and watched the women.
- Pentheus said he couldn't see them very well. His mind still boggled by Dionysus's spell, he decided it was a good idea to go to the top of a tree and look from there.
- As soon as he was at the top, the voice of Dionysus rang out, pointing out Pentheus to the

Bacchants (the followers of Dionysus).
- The god ordered his followers to punish Pentheus.
- The Bacchants went absolutely crazy. They swarmed the tree, throwing rocks and stones.
- When their attempt to climb it failed, Agave ordered them all to dig at the roots of the tree until it fell. The frenzied women clawed at the dirt and the tree toppled to the ground.
- Agave was the first to get to Pentheus.
- Yanking off his wig, Pentheus begged his mother not to hurt him.
- Agave, eyes rolling in her frenzied trance, did not recognize him. With her mouth foaming, she ripped one of her son's arms off with her bare hands.
- The other women then set upon Pentheus, tearing his skin from his bones.
- By the end, everything was covered with the King's blood.
- Agave stood triumphant, holding her son's head. The Messenger says that Agave apparently thinks it's the head of a mountain lion and is now on her way down from the mountain.

Fifth Choral Lyric

- The Chorus sings praises for the grisly death of Pentheus.
- Agave enters clutching the head of her son. She still thinks it's the head of a mountain lion.
- She brags to the Chorus about her kill and says that soon she will eat the head.
- Her voice ringing out, she calls for all of Thebes to come and see her kill.
- The deluded woman beckons for her son, Pentheus, to come and nail the lion's head to the wall. (We detect irony.)
- Cadmus enters lamenting the death of Pentheus. He describes seeing the bloody remains of his grandson strewn about the forest.
- The old man cries in shock as he sees Agave, his daughter, grasping Pentheus's head.
- Agave brags to her father about her wonderful kill.
- Cadmus weeps for the disaster that's befallen the family, pointing out that it's even worse because Dionysus was born of their own family line.
- Still not comprehending what she's done, Agave dismisses Cadmus as a grumpy old man. She wishes that her son, Pentheus, were around; he's a good hunter and would appreciate her marvelous kill. (And more irony.)
- Cadmus smacks some sense into his daughter.
- With growing horror, Agave realizes she's holding the head of her own son.
- Her father fills her in on the whole story.
- Agave and her sisters mocked Dionysus, so the god drove them crazy, sending them off into the mountains to dance and go nuts.
- Pentheus mocked Dionysus too, so he was torn apart where another family member, Actaeon, was torn apart by wild dogs.
- Cadmus wails in sorrow, for now the last of his line is dead. He was the guy who founded Thebes to begin with, and now it's all over for his family.
- Agave is wracked with grief and remorse.
- She begs her father to let her perform the last rights for her son and asks if she may kiss

each limb of his severed body.

Sixth Choral Lyric

- The Chorus celebrates the triumph of their god.

Sixth Episode

- Dionysus, no longer disguised as a mortal, appears in all his glory.
- He tells Cadmus and Agave what their fate will be.
- Cadmus, along with his wife, will be turned into a snake. He will drive a chariot and lead barbarian hordes to attack lots of Greek cities.
- Agave begs for mercy.
- Dionysus shows none and tells her she is banished from the city.
- Cadmus laments his terrible fate.
- He tells his banished daughter to go the house Aristaeus, his sister's husband.
- Sadly, Cadmus and Agave part ways.
- The Chorus sings of the power of the gods.

Themes

Theme of Man and the Natural World

Throughout *The Bacchae* there are images of humanity finding harmony with nature – ladies dancing in woods and mountains, drinking honey from the ground, breast-feeding baby animals (no, really). Of course, the play isn't just happy women prancing in the forest. We also see the destructive power that the natural world can wield – lighting, earthquakes, and man's own animal nature all take their toll on the characters in play. For more on this theme, check out "Symbolism, Imagery, Allegory" for in-depth discussions of the city vs. the wild, and man and nature in harmony.

Questions About Man and the Natural World

1. What difference exists between the way the male characters interact with nature versus the way the female characters do?
2. How are the settings of the city and the country juxtaposed by Euripides? How is this juxtaposition exemplified through human behavior?
3. How does Euripides use imagery to blur the distinction between human and animal in this play?

4. Where do you see evidence of Dionysus using nature to carry out his plan of revenge?

Chew on Man and the Natural World

Nature can be seen as a force of both destruction and creation in *The Bacchae*.

In *The Bacchae*, nature is associated with the irrational whereas civilization is associated with the rational.

Theme of Rules and Order

The Bacchae is a warning as to what can happen when an adherence to rules and order goes too far. When King Pentheus tries to impress his laws onto the ritualistic anarchy of the god Dionysus, the King, the city, and the rest of the countryside suffers. Sometimes pure law and order with no allowance for a little chaos can cause more damage than good.

Questions About Rules and Order

1. What rules are broken within this play and by whom? How does this result in chaos and ultimately, restoration?
2. Which characters in the play represent order? Which ones are associated with anarchy?
3. What distinction does the play draw between the order of the gods and the order of man?

Chew on Rules and Order

Pentheus's dedication to the laws of man neglects the much older laws of the gods.

One of the central ideas of the play is that humankind must find a way to balance its system of order with that of nature.

Theme of Religion

The central conflict of *The Bacchae* can be seen as a religious one. The god Dionysus comes home to Greece bringing with him the religion he's inspired all over Asia. When King Pentheus of Thebes refuses to worship him, the play erupts with violence. Part of what makes *The Bacchae* still timely today is its exploration of religious conflict.

Questions About Religion

1. In what ways is religion used to liberate the play's characters? How is it used to control them?
2. What similarities exist between the religious ideas of the ancient Greeks and those held within a Judeo-Christian worldview? Differences?
3. What would you say is Pentheus's religion? How does he exhibit it?

Chew on Religion
Religion is a force of anarchy in the play.

The Bacchae shows how the suppression of religious practice can ultimately unravel society.

Theme of Madness
In *The Bacchae*, the theme of madness pops up constantly. The god Dionysus has a way of driving people mad and making them wild – really wild, like ripping-their-own-children apart wild. The play could be seen of as an exploration of the bad things that can happen when the irrational and the rational aren't both allowed to exist in the lives of humanity. In other words, the play may just propose the theory: a little madness now and then is a good thing.

Questions About Madness

1. How (if at all) does madness affect punishment within this text?
2. In what way is madness linked to instinct in the play?
3. Tiresias claims that the logical-minded Pentheus is mad. Why does he say this? Do you agree? Why or why not?

Chew on Madness
The Bacchae links madness with religious ecstasy.

When Dionysus allows Agave to regain her sanity it's more of a punishment than her original madness.

Theme of Transformation
There are all kinds of transformations in *The Bacchae*. People go in and out of sanity, mild-mannered women become warrior priestesses, and stiff-necked kings become cross-dressers. And, of course, a god transforms himself into a man so as to better punish the mortals who've wronged him. All these transformations help create a series of dualities throughout the play, which perhaps connect to inherent dualities within all human beings.

Questions About Transformation

1. How does the element of disguise serve to transform characters within this piece? How do these transformations affect the play's plot?
2. Which transformations within the play are a result of personal freewill? Which are the result of a god-assigned fate? Why does the difference matter, or does it?
3. What transformations do the women in this play undergo? Agave specifically?

Chew on Transformation
Dionysus never transforms in the play, because, as a god, he exists in all forms at once.

One's transformation is inauthentic if one lacks freewill.

Theme of Violence
The Bacchae is full of gruesomeness and violence. You've got both animals and people being ripped apart. Not to mention a mother parading around with the ghastly, severed head of her own son. When watching the play we are forced to ask ourselves tough questions about violence. What is the difference between murdering and hunting? What is the meaning of blood ritual and sacrifice?

Questions About Violence

1. Beyond the entertainment value that violence offers, what purpose does it serve within the play?
2. What are some examples of passive or indirect violence within the play?
3. How is violence linked to religious practice in Dionysus's rituals?

Chew on Violence
Pentheus's dismemberment is a human sacrifice.

The Bacchae blurs the lines between murder, blood sacrifice, and killing for the purposes of hunting.

Theme of Women and Femininity
The Bacchae explores the issue of femininity in many interesting ways. We see a group of women rebel against their place in society and usurp the power of the men. Interestingly, these women don't do this of their own volition. They do so under the yoke of a male god. Of course, this male god is a little effeminate himself. It just keeps going like this. The play isn't anywhere near as cut and dried of an exploration of feminine revolt, as say, Euripides's *Medea*. With *The Bacchae*, Euripides found many new angles through which to explore the issue femininity.

Questions About Women and Femininity

1. In what ways are the female characters in the play manipulated by the male characters?
2. Do you think that the murderous mother figure exemplifies feminine strength or weakness in this piece? Why?
3. Does Pentheus exhibit any feminine stereotypes when he dresses as a woman? If so, what are they?
4. What differences do you see between the two major groups of women in the play, the Maenads and the Chorus?

Chew on Women and Femininity

The Bacchae could not be described as a play of female liberation, as all the women are subject to either a male god or the patriarchy of Pentheus.

Agave exhibits both similarities and differences to <u>Medea</u>, another of Euripides's famous murderous mothers.

Theme of Foreignness and 'the Other'

The ancient Greeks were famously suspicious of foreigners. This suspicion runs all through *The Bacchae*. The play explores the dangerous tensions that arise when a foreign religion starts to take purchase in a new land. When the cult of Dionysus meets resistance upon arrival in Greece, no end of trouble happens. What complicates the issue in the play is that the god Dionysus is Greek himself. In a way he's foreigner in his own home. The play is full of these sorts of interesting dualities.

Questions About Foreignness and 'the Other'

1. In what ways is Dionysus both Greek and foreign at the same time?
2. How do Pentheus and Dionysus each view one another as foreign? What does this say about the meaning of foreignness with regard to perspective?
3. How does the play explore what it means to feel like a foreigner in your own land?

Chew on Foreignness and 'the Other'

Pentheus exhibits typical Greek prejudice towards foreigners.

The spread of the cult of Dionysus is a foreign invasion.

Quotes

Man and the Natural World Quotes

Dionysus:
"There they sit among the rocks,
under the silvery pines--
a congregation in the open." (1)

Thought: It's significant that Dionysus drove all the women of Thebes out into the woods to celebrate his greatness. One of the central themes of the play is the tension that exists between the city of man and the natural world. Dionysus represents wild, untamed nature, so of course he'd drag the ladies out into the woods for his rituals.

Chorus:
"O Thebes, Semele's nurse
Put ivies round your turrets,
break forth in green" (3)

Thought: Did you catch the symbolism here? The Chorus invokes the image of the stone walls of Thebes being decked with greenery. It could be seen as symbolic of the relationship of man with the natural world – man being the city, nature being the ivy. Here, early in the play, the image is harmonious. Perhaps, the Chorus is still hopeful that Dionysus can bring Thebes around to his way of thinking without violence.

Dionysus:
"Touch off the thunderbolt's sizzle of light.
Burn down, oh burn down the palace of Pentheus." (93)

Thought: Now nature is not being so friendly too the those who oppose Dionysus. Whereas before we got images of nature and man in harmony, now we see nature as fearful tool of punishment. Primal nature, like Dionysus, can be both a creative and destructive force in the lives of human beings.

Pentheus:
"Ring the city round. Seal off every outlet. That's an order."
Dionysus:
"Whatever for? Can gods not somersault over walls?" (111-112)

Thought: Dionysus points out that the gods can't be contained by the man-made city. This could be seen as symbolic of the helplessness of man in the face of nature. The gods themselves represent the untamed primal forces, while the city represents the machinations of mankind.

Herdsman:
"Some [Maenads] fondled young gazelles
or untamed wolf cubs in their arms
and fed them with their own milk." (119)

Thought: Some of the women possessed by Dionysus have apparently taken to breast feeding baby animals. Kind of a strange hobby, we guess, but it's also another image of human beings and nature in harmony. The union of the Maenads and these young creatures can be seen as an intimate and holy thing.

Herdsman:
"Anyone who fancied liquid white to drink
just scratched the soil with fingertips
and got herself a jet of milk" (119)

Thought: Here we have the reverse of the previous image of the Maenads breast feeding young animals. Whereas before we saw the women nurturing nature, now we see nature nurturing the women. The possibility of true union between humanity and the natural world is shown in these complementary images.

Chorus:
"[…] a fawn at play in the green
Joy of a meadow, escaped from the […]
net […]
of the hallowing huntsman." (171)

Thought: You can find the motif of hunting throughout *The Bacchae*. It falls right into the whole man vs. nature thing, right? Humans go out into nature to shoot things and eat them. Seems pretty straightforward. This particular shout out to hunting is pretty interesting though, because it could be alluding to Pentheus who is about to get snared in Dionysus's trap. It's kind of a reversal, because throughout the play Pentheus is the main representative of the world of man, and now he'll be hunted like an animal.

Agave:
"Without a trap I trapped him:
This tenderest whelp of a lion." […]
Chorus:
"He looks like a beast of the wild with his hair." (231-246)

Thought: Throughout the play the line between man and animal is blurred. Dionysus appears in both forms, the Maenads are constantly described as animal-like, and here Agave has mistaken her own son for a lion, ripping him apart. This blurring could be seen as a way of showing that human beings are a lot more like animals than we'd like to admit, that we're not as removed from the natural world as we pretend to be.

Chorus:
"Great Dionysus, breaker of barriers
Son of the Father imperial;
Vine-clad god and priest of the natural" (308)

Thought: The Chorus celebrates Dionysus as a champion of the natural world. They highlight how he is a being that blurs the line between man and nature, bringing the opposing forces together. Sometimes this union is violent and sometimes peaceful. Whatever it takes, Dionysus seems bent on reminding humanity of its roots.

*"O Bacchus, bind us with bryony,
Crown us with ivy, and
Let every peak of Cithaeron ring
With the triumph of animal holiness." (309)*

Thought: The Chorus prays to Dionysus to bind them with nature. They long for union with both the god and the wild animal forces he represents. We would ask, at what point can this be taken too far? If all of humanity through itself headlong into animalistic practices, wouldn't we lose what it is to be human? How do we find a balance between the two forces?

Rules and Order Quotes

Dionysus:
*"Yes, here in Hellas, Thebes
is the first city I fill
with the transports of ecstatic women." (1)*

Thought: Dionysus has greatly upset the societal order of Thebes with his shenanigans. Not only has he driven people mad and sent them off to dance in the woods, but these particular people are women. This sort of behavior was totally against the rules for females in Greek society.

Tiresias:
*"No, we don't play at theologians with the gods.
We stay close to the hallowed tenets of our fathers,
old as time. Nothing can undo them ever." (19)*

Thought: Though Tiresias and Cadmus are violating the rules of the city by heading off to worship Dionysus, they are staying true to a much older set of regulations the rules of the gods. Both old men have seen enough life to know the terrible penalties that the gods put on humans who don't respect them.

Pentheus:
*"The ones [Maenads] I've rounded up, my police have handcuffed
and safely clapped in jail." (21)*

Thought: Upon his return to the city, Pentheus wastes no time trying to reassert himself. He's locking up Bacchus-crazed women left and right. Though he probably comes off as kind of a jerk, he's mostly just doing his job. What's a king to do when he comes home and finds every woman in his city dancing wildly in the woods? Isn't he expected to maintain order in the city?

Pentheus:
"From me you do not have a thing to fear.
It is never right to fume at honest men." (118)

Thought: Pentheus assures the Herdsman that it is OK for him to tell the whole story of the Maenads even if it the tale contains things the King doesn't want to hear. Though he seems to come off as angry and closed minded for most of the play, this hints that he previously ran Thebes in a pretty rational and even-tempered way. It's only towards anarchy of Dionysus that he gets all cranky. It seems that Pentheus is a man who greatly values order.

Herdsman:
"They [Maenads] tore like an invading army
through the villages [...]
They snatched up babies out of homes.
They carried fire on their flowing heads and it did not burn them." (119)

Thought: Looks like Pentheus has got a full-blown case of anarchy going on. Once you've got baby snatching and flaming-headed ladies running round, there's no denying it. By trying to suppress the celebrations of the Maenads he's caused disorder in the entire countryside.

Dionysus:
"I'm your lady's maid." [...]
Pentheus:
"There you dress it. I'm all yours now."
Dionysus:
"Tch! Tch! Your girdles loose,
And your skirts all uneven at the ankles." (183-185)

Thought: Here, both Dionysus and Pentheus are taking on feminine roles. Dionysus play acts at being a lady in waiting, while Pentheus acts like a straight up princess. This blurring of the lines between male and female is another example of the way that Dionysus shatters the carefully ordered social structure of Thebes.

Chorus:
"Let Justice sworded walk
To strike through the throat and kill
this godless ruthless lawless man" (211)

Thought: It's interesting that the Chorus describes Pentheus as lawless. He'd probably say the same the thing about them. The Chorus, like Tiresias and Cadmus, adhere to a different set of laws than Pentheus – the laws of the divine.

Leader:
"Tell it all. Explain exactly how he died--
this perverse man, this purveyor of perversion." (224)

Thought: Pentheus constantly accuses the Bacchants of perverting the order of society, with their crazed revelries. Here, however, we see the Chorus call him the pervert. They see Pentheus's lack of fealty to Dionysus as the true perversion of what is right and good.

Pentheus:
"Have mercy on me, Mother,
and because of my mistakes do not kill your son--your son." (225)

Thought: Many Greek tragedies center around the violation of a pretty fundamental law. One of the most popular no-no's for a tragedian to write about was one family member killing another. Oedipus killed his father. Clytemnestra killed her husband. Orestes killed his mother. The list goes on. In *The Bacchae* we have a mother killing her son. What's interesting is that this horrific act is god sanctioned, and in fact isn't the choice of the mother at all. What makes it even more messed up is that Dionysus himself is related to these people. Pentheus is his cousin and Agave is his aunt.

Dionysus:
"My father sanctioned this [punishment] in ages past, great Zeus." (316)

Thought: In the end, it is the will of the gods that is triumphant. The rules and laws of man prove to insignificant in the face of the gods' ancient decrees. Pentheus brings his entire household to ruin by attempting place his own idea of order over that of Dionysus.

Religion Quotes

Dionysus:
"You see, they should have […] known better
[…] my mother's sisters,
who said that I, Dionysus, was no son of Zeus" (1)

Thought: That's the understatement of the century. The fact that his mortal relatives deny that Dionysus is actually a god is the conflict brewing at the heart of the play. All the horrible blood and mayhem that we see is a result of this religious difference.

Cadmus:
"I'm all ready, see,
complete in Dionysiac trappings.
And why not?
He's my own daughter's child" (8)

Thought: Wouldn't it be a little weird if one of your relatives was a god? That's the situation that old Cadmus is in. Here we see him embracing the new religion of his grandson. Unlike Pentheus and the rest of his family, Cadmus totally buys into the divinity of Dionysus. Of course, this doesn't help at all by the end of the play. He's punished too.

Pentheus:
"She'd [Semele] had the nerve to name Zeus the Father
as her lover…What gall! What effrontery!" (21)

Thought: Notice that Pentheus is not blasphemous towards all gods. It's just Dionysus that he has a problem with. He is offended by the idea that Semele, his aunt and Dionysus' mother, was the lover of Zeus. Perhaps this shows a dedication to Zeus, the Greek king of the gods. In the Greek mind, however, it was important to pay homage to all gods, because anyone of them could deal out punishment.

Tiresias:
"He [Dionysus] is a god of prophecies […]
He also has assumed some of Ares' duties
A regiment in arms, for instance" (22)

Thought: To the ancient Greeks, it was totally cool for gods to share duties. It seems that Dionysus is now influencing both prophecy, which was previously an Apollo thing, and war, which was mostly Ares's job before that.

Pentheus:
"Rituals of possession of ? Of what particular form? […]
You make me want to hear." (42-46)

Thought: Pentheus seems really interested in the particulars of a religion that he claims is a load of garbage. Is he really as sure of the falseness of Dionysus as he says he is? In any case, it's this curiosity that eventually leads him to his grisly death.

Herdsman:
"great lordly bulls,
one minute glaring in all the pride of their horns,
the next dragged to ground like carcasses
by the swarming hands of girls." (119)

Thought: One the symbols of Dionysus was the bull. Later in the play he even appears to Pentheus as one. Given that, it's interesting that it was also common for bulls to be sacrificed in his rituals.

Herdsman:
"After all this my lord,
whoever this city be you must receive him in our city.
He is powerful in many things." (119)

Thought: The Herdsman has witnessed the raw power of Dionysus and wisely advises
Pentheus to pay honor to the god. Of course, the King refuses. We wonder what has turned
Pentheus so steadfastly against Dionysus. Is it just that their philosophies of life are so
different? Is Pentheus jealous that his cousin was born a god and not him?

Chorus:
"Slowly but surely divine
Power moves to annul
The brutally minded man
Who in his wild delusions refuses
To reverence the gods." (173)

Thought: A constant theme throughout Greek tragedy is the price men pay for blasphemy. In
play after play, we see heroes and heroines punished for disrespect to the gods. It's interesting
that the theme figured so prominently in this play by Euripides, who some scholars believe was
an atheist.

Chorus:
"As to the rest, the sublime is simple and leads
To a beautiful life, [...]
It sheds from it everything wrong
In pursuit of the right a
And homage to heaven." (212)

Thought: The Chorus sings a song of devotion to the divine. To them, the life they've chosen is
the true path to the sublime. They've given up everything for their god, shedding everything in
the name of Dionysus.

Agave:
"But gods should not repeat the passions of mere men." (315)

Thought: Yeah, maybe, but this doesn't seem to be true at all with the gods of the ancient
Greeks. They act pretty much exactly like people. They betray each other, fight amongst
themselves, and fall in love. The only real difference is that they have a ton of power. It's really
no wonder the Greeks were busy trying to be humble all the time. With the world of the divine in
such tumult all the time, you had to be really careful not to anger any divine entity.

Madness Quotes

Dionysus:
"my mother's sisters [...]
I've driven from their wits and from their homes:
out the mountains and out of their minds." (1)

Thought: Dionysus's first act of punishment is to drive all his mother's sisters crazy for denying the fact that he is a god. Ironically, the people who have denied his divinity are now out celebrating it. It makes sense that Dionysus would choose such a punishment, since he was thought to represent the irrational.

Chorus:
"the rounded timbrel [...]
They gave it in the hand of
Mother Rhea to drum-beat
For shouting Bacchants raving.
The run-mad satyrs snatched it,
Joined it to the dances" (4)

Thought: A little madness now and then is a good thing. At least, that's what your average Bacchant would tell you. Wild frenzies are an essential part of their rituals. Some scholars say that the main message of *The Bacchae* is to show how it's important for humans to allow space for irrational to exist in their lives.

Tiresias:
"There is no cure for madness
when the cure itself is mad." (22)

Thought: The seer, Tiresias, is chastising Pentheus for not honoring Dionysus. Pentheus has been arguing that all the new god's crazy rituals are just that – crazy. Tiresias is trying to tell him that denying the madness that Dionysus brings is itself a crazy idea. One of the central ideas of the play seems to be the importance of finding balance between the irrational and the rational.

Herdsman:
"Oh sir, I've seen the raving ladies--
those who streamed out from their homes stung mad,
their white limbs flashing." (117)

Thought: What is sanity? What is madness? What's the difference between the two? When we read *The Bacchae* we really start to question.

Pentheus:
"So,
like a wildfire it already hurries here,
outrageously, this mass hysteria,
disgracing us before the whole of Thebes." (121)

Thought: By trying to repress the madness of Dionysus's rituals, Pentheus has allowed the entire land to erupt with hysteria. Once again we see demonstrated in the play the dangers of totally suppressing rationality. If you try to bury that part of the human mind it all might just explode in your face.

Dionysus:
"Sane, he [Pentheus] will never consent
to put women's clothing on,
but once deranged he will." (119)

Thought: This seem a little inconsistent to us. Dionysus says this after Pentheus has already left the stage to dress like a woman. Does this mean that the god already put the spell of Pentheus before he left, or is it a glitch in the logic of the script?

Chorus:
"Slowly but surely divine
Power moves to annul
The brutally minded man
Who in his wild delusions refuses
To reverence the gods." (173)

Thought: Here the Chorus alludes that to deny the gods is madness. It's interesting that the people telling us this worship a god who induces madness as a hobby. Looks like no matter what you do in the world of *The Bacchae* you end up crazy.

Pentheus:
"Now I'd say your head was horned…
or were you an animal all the while?
For certainly you've changed…oh, into a bull." […]
Dionysus: "You see things as you ought." (178-179)

Thought: Now that Dionysus has messed with Pentheus's head the beguiled King can finally see the truth of the god's form. Does that mean Pentheus was crazy before or that he's crazy now?

Messenger:
"She was foaming at the mouth.
Her eyes dilated rolled.
Her mind was gone--possessed by Bacchus--
she could not hear her son." (225)

Thought: Talk about madness. Agave has been driven so insane by Dionysus that she's about rip her own son limb from limb. She is in the throws of a holy trance, which, depending how you look at it, has some very holy or very unholy results.

Agave:
"I seem to be becoming…somehow…aware.
Something in my mind is changing. […]
No…no…It's Pentheus' head I hold…
most wretched woman!" (284)

Thought: As Agave finally comes out of her Bacchus-induced trance, she realizes the horrible thing she's done. She would've been a lot happier if she'd been allowed to stay filled with the mad ecstasy of Bacchus forever. What do you think this might be saying of the nature of madness?

Transformation Quotes

Dionysus:
"I am changed, of course, a god made man" (1)

Thought: There are lots of transformations that happen in *The Bacchae*. The first one happens before the play even begins. Dionysus has changed his appearance to that of a mortal. We wonder why he feels the need to do so. Couldn't he just show up all godly glory and start punishing the unbelievers? Maybe, he's testing them, or maybe he just likes messing with people. What do you think?

Pentheus:
"Something very strange is happening in this town.
They tell me our womenfolk have left their homes
--in ecstasy if you please-- […]
dancing honor on this brash new god." (21)

Thought: King Pentheus is furious about the little transformation that Dionysus has performed on the women of Thebes. They've gone from submissive ladies, totally under his control, to wild women of the woods. It probably gets under his skin even more this wild group of women includes his mother and aunts.

Dionysus:
"Face to face...he [himself] gave the rituals of possession." (41)

Thought: Here Dionysus, in disguise, hints to Pentheus of his frenzied rituals. When the spirit of Dionysus possesses people they are certainly transformed. The frenzy of the Bacchants bring them closer to their god.

Herdsman:
"They carried fire on their flowing heads and it did not burn them.[...]
spearpoints drew no blood" (119)

Thought: The Maenads now seem to have undergone an even greater transformation. They started out as mild-mannered housewives. Then they were crazed worshipers. Now Dionysus has turned them into warrior women of almost god-like powers.

Dionysus:
"We'll go inside and I'll dress you up myself."
Pentheus:
"What kind of dress? A female's?" (152-153)

Thought: Dionysus's makeover session with King Pentheus is yet another example of transformation in *The Bacchae*. This one is pretty ironic to say the least. Just a little while ago Pentheus was busting on Dionysus for looking effeminate, now the King is the dressing like a woman.

Dionysus:
"A thyrsus in your [Pentheus'] hand, and a spotted fawn skin on." (160)

Thought: Not only is Dionysus making Pentheus over as a woman, he's also dressing him up like a Bacchant. The thyrsus, an ivy covered staff, and fawn skin are key pieces to the uniform of your average worshiper of Dionysus. This part of the transformation is just as ironic women's clothing, as Pentheus has done nothing but resist and deny the spreading religion of Dionysus.

Pentheus:
"Now I'd say your head was horned...
or were you an animal all the while?
For certainly you've changed...oh, into a bull." [...]
Dionysus: "You see things as you ought." (178-179)

Thought: Though Pentheus speculates that the guy he thought was just a priest of Dionysus has changed into a bull, there's really been no transformation at all – at least on Dionysus' end. It's Pentheus's perception that has transformed. Now the King perceives Dionysus in one of his other forms a bull. Does this mean that gods exist in all their forms at once? As such, do they ever transform? When humans think they do, is it really just their perception that has shifted?

Dionysus:
"The sins of jealousy and anger
made this Pentheus deal unjustly with one bringing blessings." (310)

Thought: Dionysus pronounces this as he appears at the end of the play no longer disguised as a mortal. He's appearing in his godly form to deal out judgment onto the mortals who've wronged him.

Dionysus:
"As to you Cadmus,
you shall be changed into a snake." (310)

Thought: Part of Cadmus's fate is to be transformed into a snake. We wonder what the significance is of this specific animal. Could it be related to the snakes that the Maenads wrap in their hair?

Violence Quotes
Dionysus:
"If the town of Thebes becomes inflamed
and tries to oust my Maenads from the mountains,
I shall go out there myself
and lead my Bacchants in battle." (1)

Thought: From the very beginning there is a threat of violence in the play. Dionysus swears not to take any disrespect from Thebes, and he proves himself to be true to his words. This statement from Dionysus is the first hint of all the terror that is to come.

Soldier:
"The animal [Dionysus] we found was tame, sir:
put himself without resistance in our hands" (31)

Thought: Dionysus doesn't put up a fight when he's caught by Pentheus's men. Though he's capable of obliterating them all without any effort, he casually walks into Thebes. We wonder why he bothers with the deception. Could he be luring Pentheus into a sense of complacency? What do you think?

Herdsman:
"You could see a woman with a bellowing calf
actually in her grip, tearing it apart. [...]
ribs and cloven hooves
being tossed high and low;
and blood-smeared members dangling from the pines" (119)

Thought: OK, here comes the violence. The Maenads enact their rage at the intrusion of the Herdsman and his buddies by ripping apart the men's cattle. This horrific dismembering could also be seen as a sacrifice to Dionysus.

Herdsman:
"The villagers [...]
took up arms against the manic ones [Maenads]
Then what a spectacle, my king, how sinister!
Their spear points drew no blood!" (119)

Thought: The villagers are completely defenseless in the face of the Maenads. When they try to meet the crazed women's violence with violence, they only bring more destruction on themselves. It seems there is no fighting with the will of the gods.

Dionysus:
"you must not take up arms against a god." (122)

Thought: No kidding. Dionysus, in the form of the Stranger, warns Pentheus again and again not to try and use violence against Dionysus's followers. It's the same thing as trying to strike at Dionysus himself. The central spine of *The Bacchae* is a chain of increasingly violent reactions from the god and his followers against Pentheus's blasphemies.

Pentheus:
"a most appropriate sacrifice
women's blood and massacre in the glens of Cithaeron." (125)

Thought: The King seems to be fully prepared to slaughter all of Maenads. Wait, aren't they his own people? Aren't his mother and aunts the leaders? It seems that Pentheus's obsessive refusal to accept the ways of Dionysus has turned him into a real monster.

Dionysus:
"Pentheus murdered in his mother's grasp
will come to know full well at last
Dionysus, son of Zeus, a god indeed" (170)

Thought: Dionysus lays his plan for punishment right out there. When Pentheus dies at the hands of his own mother it's no surprise. Of course, Euripides didn't risk ruining the ending for his audience since they all knew the myth anyway. The harsh violence of Pentheus's death is still pretty shocking, though, once the playwright gets done describing the grisly details. In ancient Greek tragedies, it was not what happened that the audiences came to see, but how it happened.

Messenger:
"Gripping his left hand and forearm
and purchasing her foot against the doomed man's ribs,
she dragged his arm off at the shoulder" (225)

Thought: Not only is Pentheus killed by his own mother, but he is also literally ripped apart. The horrific violence of this act is a punishment for both of them. It's also a spiritual act. Just as earlier in the play cattle were dismembered in the name of Bacchus, now a human being is sacrificed for the sake of the god.

Agave:
"Celebrate my hunting prowess." [...]
Cadmus:
"Murder is what your tragic hands have done.
Beautiful the victim cut down by the gods:
the sacrificial feast you call me to and Thebes." (263)

Thought: Here we have the same violent act of Agave dismembering her son described in three different ways. Agave calls it hunting, while Cadmus relates it to murder and sacrifice. What's the difference between the three acts do you think? How do you separate one from the other?

Cadmus:
"he [Cadmus] must lead barbarian mongrel hordes against our Hellas" (319)

Thought: Cadmus is doomed to live a life of violence. He must lead foreign soldiers in battles against other Greeks. We wonder why this particular fate was put on the old man. It doesn't quite seem to have the same ironic twist as the rest of the play. Some scholars think that this ending was added in later years after Euripides's death, which would explain its incongruity.

Women and Femininity Quotes

Dionysus:
"every female in this city,
I've started on a wild stampede from home" (1)

Thought: *The Bacchae* could be interpreted by some as a text of female liberation. Greek women were pretty much expected to stay home and be submissive. Not so with these ladies of Thebes. They're all out dancing in the woods. It's interesting, however, that these women aren't rebelling because they thought it was a good idea. Instead, they've been magically driven to it, and by a male god. They've unwillingly become the Maenads, the frenzied worshipers of Dionysus.

Dionysus:
"Onwards! My women Tmolus, you bulwark of Lydia,
you, my sisterhood of worshipers
whom I led from foreign lands to be my company
in rest and march..." (1)

Thought: The Chorus, unlike the Maenads, celebrates Dionysus of their own choice. Their presence in Thebes must be very disconcerting to Pentheus and the men of Thebes. They are strong, powerful women with the power of a god behind them. These ladies are completely outside of the patriarchal power structure of Thebes.

Chorus
"Him [Dionysus] who his mother miscarried in a blast of light from Zeus, [...]
Was taken by Zeus and sheltered within his thigh:
Stitched with golden brackets,
Secreted from Hera." (2)

Thought: Here's an interesting inversion of the role woman. Dionysus began as a fetus in the womb of his mother, Semele. But when his father, Zeus, accidentally destroyed Semele he stitched Dionysus' fetus into his leg until Dionysus was ready to be born. In a way, Dionysus was given birth to twice – once by a male, once by a female. Throughout the play, we see this blurring of the lines between the sexes.

Pentheus:
"Hm, my man--not a bad figure, eh?
At least for the ladies; [...]
Nice ringlets, too...
no good for wrestling, though" (32)

Thought: The King compares the human form that Dionysus has taken to a woman. This is undoubtedly meant to demean the man that Pentheus thinks is just some foreign priest. The fact that being called effeminate is an insult is indicative of the low status of women in ancient Greek society. Of course, calling somebody a girly man isn't usually a compliment these days either, is it?

Herdsman:
"Some [Maenads] lying on their backs upon the piney needles,
All modestly, not as you suggested, sir,
not in their cups, or in a flute-induced trance,
or any wildwood chase of love." (119)

Thought: The Herdsman corrects Pentheus's assumption that the Maenads are going around sleeping with everybody. If Pentheus were right about all the women acting loose, it would be a big no-no. Part of the suppression of women in ancient Greek was sexual. Wives were expected to stay at home and behave themselves, while men had a lot more freedom.

Herdsman:
"Oh, the women wounded men, set men to flight…
that was not without some unknown power." (119)

Thought: It would've been hard for a ancient Greek male to believe that a woman could defeat a man in battle, as women were considered much weaker.

Pentheus:
"Well, how do I look?
Don't I have Aunt Ino's air,
and Agave my mother's carriage?" (180)

Thought: The beguiled, cross-dressing Pentheus seems to proud of his new found feminine beauty. Don't miss the irony of him comparing himself to his mother, the lady who's just about rip him limb from limb in a few pages. When this happens it could be seen as an inversion of stereotypical gender roles. Agave becomes the violent aggressor, while Pentheus becomes the helpless victim.

Pentheus:
"Have mercy on me, Mother,
and because of my mistakes do not kill your son--your son." (225)

Thought: A mother killing her own son could be seen as a rejection of motherhood itself. Agave gave Pentheus life and now she is taking it away. This isn't the first time we see a mother killing her son in work of Euripides. Check out our guide to *Medea* for another example.

Agave:
"come and see our catch:
the animal we Cadmean daughters caught and killed…
and not with nets or thronged Thessalian spears
but our own strong white hands." (259)

Thought: Agave and the other Maenads have taken on yet another traditionally male role. Earlier in the play they became warriors, and now they've become hunters as well. It's interesting that this happened through possession by a male god. Of course, Dionysus himself is said to be a bit effeminate, existing somewhere between male and female. Perhaps this blurring of the lines between the sexes is a way to bring human beings closer to him.

Agave:
"I've deserted loom and shuttle
and gone on to greater things
to wild beast hunting with bare hands." (261)

Thought: This statement seems to point out how deeply entrenched patriarchy, or male domination, was in ancient Greek society. Agave is proud of the fact that she's deserted "womanly" duties and has taken on "manly" ones. Weren't both roles equally as valuable and necessary to society?

Agave:
"I seem to be becoming…somehow…aware.
Something in my mind is changing. […]
No…no…It's Pentheus' head I hold…
most wretched woman!" (284)

Thought: Agave's final transformation yields an unpleasant surprise. She's now gone from triumphant warrior priestess to a murderer. To make matters worse, she's murdered her own child. What's interesting about Agave's case is that her transformations have existed only in the realm of her own perception.

Foreignness and 'the Other' Quotes

Dionysus:
"All Asia is mine, […]
But in the land of Hellas
this city Thebes is the is the first place I have visited." (1)

Thought: In case you don't know, Hellas is another word for Greece. Dionysus is pointing out here that he's spread his religion all over Asia, but that Thebes is the first city in Greece to get a taste of his lively rituals. By Euripides's time, Dionysus was a considered a totally legit god, but back in the day, the religion probably seemed like a bizarre foreign invader.

Dionysus:
Onwards! My women of Tmolus, you bulwark of Lydia,
you, my sisterhood of worshipers,
whom I led from foreign lands" (1)

Thought: *The Bacchae* is full of dualities and paradoxes. Here's one of them. Dionysus is the son of a Greek woman and a Greek god. Though he's Greek through and through, his religion and his battalion of followers come from Asia. In a way, Dionysus is native and foreign at the same time.

Chorus:
"From the purlieus of Asia I come
Deserting Tmolus the holy." (2)

Thought: The ladies of the Chorus have left everything they know for Dionysus. He's plucked them from their homeland on the mountain of Tmolus and taken them to a foreign land to spread their religion. The fact that they've come so far from home shows the depth of their devotion.

Tiresias:
"He [Dionysus] is was who turned the grape into a flowing draft
and proffered it to mortals;
so when they fill themselves with liquid vine
they put an end to grief." (22)

Thought: Interesting fact: wine is a foreigner to Europe. That seems strange, right? Europe is famous for its many different kinds of wine. It is a fact, though, that the grape is not a native fruit to Europe. It came from Asia way back in the day. *The Bacchae* is, in part, a celebration of that highly successful foreigner invasion.

Pentheus:
"Foreigners have much less sense than Greeks." (54)

Thought: Pentheus here exhibits a common attitude in ancient Greece. He pretty much thinks Greeks are the smartest, most civilized people on Earth. We can't be too hard on him, though. We have a feeling that the people on the other side of the sea feel the same way about themselves, and think the Greeks are backwards and uncivilized. Suspicion of foreigners and the unknown in general is a pretty common human trait.

Leader:
"Oh, let me shout my song in foreign tunes:
a foreigner who need no longer tremble in fear of fetters." (220)

Thought: Now that Pentheus has been killed, the Chorus need no longer fear his persecution. Their foreign religion has conquered the over the stubborn Greek King.

Agave:
"Bacchants from Asia, look!" (228)

Thought: This is the only time in the play that one of the Maenads, the Theban women whom Dionysus incites to worship him, meets Chorus, the god's Asian followers. It's interesting how Euripides places these two groups of women in contrast with each other. The Chorus worships Dionysus of their own volition, while the Greek women were forced into it. What does this say about the spreading of this foreign religion in Greece?

Dionysus:
"I shall not curb the flail
under which these culprits have to smart
They shall be exiled from the city [...]
Not one of them shall ever see their fatherland again." (310)

Thought: Exile was a fate worse than death for most ancient Greeks. For many, their entire sense of self was based around whichever city they lived in. Perhaps, their suspicion of foreigners was heightened by their fierce loyalty to their own homeland.

Dionysus:
"You [Cadmus] shall drive a chariot drawn by bullocks [...]
leading a barbarian tribe." (310)

Thought: Part of Cadmus's punishment is that he must lead an army of foreigners in a series of battles. Notice the use of the word barbarian here. To the ancient Greeks, most every foreigner was barbaric. It's extra humiliating for Cadmus to lead a group of people who he feels are inferior.

Cadmus:
"an old man as an alien, his home in alien lands.[...]
he must lead barbarian mongrel hordes against our Hellas" (319)

Thought: So, not only must Cadmus lead an army of foreigners in battle, but he also must lead them in attacking other Greeks. It really is a fate worse than death for they guy who founded Thebes. He's about as Greek as it gets, and now he's being forced to betray his own people.

Plot Analysis

Classic Plot Analysis

Initial Situation
Dionysus swears punishment.
Dionysus fills us in on all we need to know at the beginning of the play. The god comes out and launches into a monologue that gives us some exposition (back-story) about his bizarre birth. He then proceeds to let us know that he intends to punish all the folks in Thebes who say he's not a god. The first on his list are his mother's relatives, members of the house of Cadmus, the ruling family of Thebes. The stage is set for mortals to feel some godly wrath.

Conflict
Dionysus toys with Pentheus.
Pentheus shows up super angry, because all the women of Thebes, including his own mother, are out in the woods doing crazy rituals in honor of Dionysus. He arrests the Stranger, a guy he thinks is the leader of the Dionysian cult. Unfortunately for Pentheus, the Stranger is really Dionysus in disguise. The conflict gets revved up when Dionysus summons lightning and an earthquake to warn Pentheus against his blasphemy.

Complication
Dionysus convinces Pentheus to spy on the Maenads.
The conflict between Dionysus and Pentheus takes an interesting turn when Dionysus convinces the King to go spy on the rituals of the Maenads. The best part is that the straight laced Pentheus must do this while wearing women's clothes.

Climax
Pentheus is violently dismembered by his own mother.
The play reaches a grisly peak with the death of King Pentheus. A Messenger tells us all about how Agave, Pentheus's mother, ripped her son's body apart with her bare hands while he was spying on the Maenads.

Suspense
Agave returns bearing Pentheus's head.
Agave marches back to Thebes bearing the bloody head of Pentheus. The Dionysus-enchanted woman is under the impression that it's a lion's head she's carrying. There's all kinds of suspense as the audience watches Agave slowly come to her senses. It's horrific when she figures out she's really holding the head of her son.

Denouement
Dionysus sentences Cadmus and Agave.
Things begin to wind down as Dionysus appears and deals out punishments, banishing Agave and cursing Cadmus.

Conclusion
Dionysus is triumphant.
The play wraps up with Cadmus and Agave walking off to their fates. Dionysus hovers above, reveling in his godly glory.

Booker's Seven Basic Plots Analysis: Tragedy

Anticipation Stage
Dionysus declares that he will punish Thebes for denying his divinity.
Dionysus sets the stage for tragedy when he determines to punish the house of Cadmus for denying his godliness. He takes over the minds of the women of Thebes, driving them to dance around in the mountains, worshiping him. This causes King Pentheus to lash out against the god. It's clear, as the two sides square off against each other, that some serious craziness is about to go down.

Dream Stage
Dance party!
At first Dionysus's retaliation against the house of Cadmus seems pretty harmless. All the women are out dancing in the woods. Cadmus and Tiresias put on some fawn skins and do some dancing of their own. Overall, the play has a light and playful feel. This, however will not last.

Frustration Stage
Arresting Dionysus is a bad idea.
When the obstinate King Pentheus starts to crack down on the Dionysian uprising, things start to get ugly. Some of his men disturb the Maenads' woodland revelries and the ladies go crazy, ravaging the countryside. When Pentheus arrests Dionysus, who is in disguise as a mortal, things start to get really raw. Dionysus summons earthquake and lightning to destroy his jail and lacerate the palace.

Nightmare Stage
Pentheus dismembered.
Nightmarish doesn't even describe it. Dionysus convinces Pentheus to go spy on the Maenads, telling the King that he'll be safe if he's disguised in women's clothes. Then the god betrays the King and points him out to his followers. Pentheus ends up being ripped apart by his own mother, Agave, on of the Maenads. The rest of the crazed women finish the job, tearing at his flesh and throwing it in the air.

Destruction or Death Wish Stage
Dionysus triumphant.
Maddened Agave returns to Thebes, clutching the bloody head of her son, under the false impression that it is the head of a lion. The audience is moved to fear and pity as they watch her slowly realize the terrible thing she's done. Dionysus appears in all his godly glory and punishes Cadmus and Agave. *The Bacchae*, is different from a lot of tragedies in that it doesn't tell the story of a tragic hero's downfall. We don't find our hero, Dionysus, suffering and

bemoaning his fate at the end of the play. Instead, it's everybody else that suffers.

Three Act Plot Analysis

Act I
The first act begins with Dionysus declaring that he's in the midst of punishing the house of Cadmus for denying that he's a god. He's taken over the minds of the women of Thebes and sent them off to the woods to dance in celebration of him. We know there's going to be serious trouble when King Pentheus returns and swears to squash this Dionysian uprising.

Act II
The conflict between Pentheus and Dionysus continues to drive the play. Some of Pentheus's men try to grab his mother Agave from the rituals. This causes her and the other Maenads to ravage the countryside. Meanwhile Pentheus tries to imprison the Stranger, who is really Dionysus in disguise. The act peaks when the god summons earthquakes and lightning, squashing the stable where the King tried to imprison him in.

Act III
The final act is propelled forward when Dionysus convinces Pentheus that he should check out the Maenads rituals for himself. The King dresses as a woman to disguise himself. This does him no good at all and he is ripped apart by his own mother. The play peaks as maddened Agave returns bearing her son's head and slowly realizes exactly what she's done. Euripides wraps the play up with Dionysus dealing out punishments to Agave and Cadmus.

Study Questions

1. What is the difference between murder, hunting, and sacrifice?
2. What is the greater meaning of all of the dualities in the play?
3. What would the play be like if Agave were the protagonist? Cadmus? The Herdsman?
4. What is madness in the play? What is sanity?
5. Directors often set Greek tragedies in another place and time other than ancient Greece. If you were directing *The Bacchae*, where and when would you choose to set the play? How would your choice inform the play?

Characters

All Characters

Dionysus Character Analysis

Dionysus, the protagonist of *The Bacchae*, is one big contradiction. The character embodies many of the dualities that we see throughout the play. Let's take a look at some of these. First of all, in some ways he represents both human and god. Sure Dionysus definitely has all the powers of a god. We definitely see plenty of evidence of this. This guy summons earthquakes, lightning, and has a knack for getting into peoples heads, driving them totally insane. Still though, part of him is human. Though his father was Zeus, King of the gods, his mother was the mortal woman, Semele. Also, for most of the play, he appears in his human disguise, the Stranger. Though, Dionysus is a god through and through, it seems like Euripides manages to in some ways tie him to the mortal world as well.

Another interesting duality is that Dionysus is foreign and Greek at the same time. He was born in Greece, but his religion, for some reason, first spread in Asia. In his opening monologue he tells the audience, "All Asia is mine", but that "In the land of Hellas [Greece] this city Thebes is first place I have visited." Dionysus has come home to Thebes, the place of his birth, to spread his religion and to punish the members of his mortal family who have denied his divinity. He is not surrounded not by Greek followers, but with a chorus of Asian women. Even the mortal form he takes looks Asian instead of Greek. In a way, though Dionysus has returned to his hometown, he's totally foreign.

Yet another contradiction is that Dionysus in some ways represents both male and female. Yes, he is a male god, but the mortal form he takes is said to be quite effeminate. When Pentheus sees him for the first time he says, "Hm, my man – not a bad figure, eh? At least for the ladies" (32). The King goes on to tell Dionysus that he has "nice ringlets," and that they're "very fetching […] the way they ripple round [his] cheeks" (32). Also, notice that all of Dionysus's followers are women. The Chorus is made up of his female Asian followers, and the Maenads are all the women of Thebes. We should also note Dionysus's strange birth. After his mother was obliterated, Zeus stitched Dionysus's fetus into his thigh until the baby was ready to be born. In a way, Dionysus was born of both male and female. Looks like from the get-go there was some blurring of gender centered around Dionysus.

Last of all, we'd like to point out that Dionysus is both animal and human. When Dionysus puts Pentheus into a trance, the King observes the god's animal form saying, "Now I'd say your head was horned…or were you an animal all the while? For certainly you've turned into a bull" (178). Also, the Chorus describes their god in animal terms, singing, "Appear as a bull or be seen as many-headed dragon. Or come as a fire-breathing vision of a lion." This duality of animal and man, could be seen as a duality within a duality. By taking both forms, Dionysus has one foot in nature and one in civilization. In a way he's a bridge between the two forces. Also, he's a bridge between the animalistic irrational forces and that of the very human rational forces. While he causes a lot of chaos in the play, every time he's in his human form in the play, he's cool, calm, and collected.

So, what's with all these dualities? Perhaps the play is trying to say that everything that exists is also its opposite at the very same time – more specifically, that we as human beings are inherently contradicted. We're all both rational and irrational. All humans are animals, but there's also something special that undeniably separates us from the rest of Earth's living creatures. Though we all (or at least most of us) belong to one gender or another, there are things about all of us that don't quite fit into the role that society prescribes to specific sexes. Even though everybody is from somewhere, we're all a foreigner somewhere else. Sometimes we even become foreigners in our own homes. Lastly, even though we're certainly mortal, maybe, just maybe, some part of us is eternal and divine. It seems to us, that in the character of Dionysus, Euripides captured many of the amazing contradictions that make up every human being.

Dionysus Timeline and Summary

- Appears in Thebes disguised as the mortal, Stranger.
- Monologues about the history of his birth.
- Informs us that he's come from Asia to spread his religion.
- Says that he's possessed the women of Thebes to punish them for blasphemy.
- Lets himself be arrested by Pentheus.
- Summons lightning and earthquakes to smash his jail.
- Teases his followers for doubting him.
- Convinces Pentheus that he must dress up in women's clothing to observe the Maenads.
- Beguiles Pentheus so that the King can see his bull form.
- Leads the cross-dressed Pentheus through Thebes to humiliate him.
- Takes Pentheus out to spy on the Maenads.
- Helps Pentheus climb to the top of a pine tree.
- Illuminates the sky so that Pentheus is exposed.
- Orders the Maenads to rip Pentheus apart.
- Shows up in all his godly glory.
- Curses Cadmus to lead barbarian hordes in the form of a snake.
- Banishes Agave from Thebes.
- Chastises them both for not worshipping him to begin with.

King Pentheus Character Analysis

Pentheus is not a typical Greek antagonist. Sure he's the guy that stands in the way of our hero and protagonist, Dionysus, making him a shoe-in for job. In a lot of ways, though, he more closely resembles a tragic hero than Dionysus does, at least according to Aristotle. For one, Pentheus has a clear *hamartia*. This word is most commonly translated as "tragic flaw," but is more accurately described as an "error in judgment" or a "missing of the mark."

The King makes the error of errors by trying to defy the god Dionysus. This big old mistake results in the King being ripped limb from limb by his Bacchus-crazed mother, Agave. A Messenger reports that just before Agave had her bloody way with Pentheus, he pleaded, "Have mercy on me, Mother, and because of my mistakes don't kill your son" (225). Did you catch the key word there? Pentheus admits to making a "mistake." Yep, sounds like a *hamartia* to us.

As Pentheus admits to doing wrong, he's also exhibiting another tell-tale sign of a tragic hero: an *anagnorisis*. This is when a character has a recognition or realization of some kind. Not that it does him much good. The Messenger tells us that immediately after Agave "dragged his arm off his shoulder," while the rest of the Maenads "shredded his limbs" and threw his skin around "like a ball" (225). Looks like in the world of Euripides it doesn't much matter if somebody realizes they did wrong or not. Everybody's doomed anyway.

It's pretty easy to dislike Pentheus. The dude is kind of a stuffed shirt, and a total party pooper. When Agave and the other women of Thebes run off into the mountains to dance, drink wine, and praise Dionysus, Pentheus does everything he can to squelch the revelry. We'd also like to point out, however, that Pentheus is just doing his job. What's a King supposed do when he comes home and everybody's gone totally crazy? What kind of King would he be if he let anarchy take over his fair city? You could choose to view Pentheus as just your average ordinary King caught up in very extraordinary situation.

King Pentheus Timeline and Summary

- Returns to Thebes upon hearing rumors of the upheaval.
- Talks a lot of junk about Dionysus.
- Chastises Tiresias and Cadmus for going off to worship Dionysus.
- Orders his men to mess up Tiresias's house.
- Also orders that the Stranger from Lydia (really Dionysus) be arrested.
- Criticizes/admires the Stranger's feminine looks.
- Tries to find out what the Dionysus's rituals are really like.
- Locks up the Stranger.
- Freaks out when the Stranger escapes, amidst earthquake and lightning.
- Threatens to kill all the Bacchants.
- Agrees to dress up like a woman to spy on the Maenads
- Is beguiled by Dionysus.
- Worries about his own feminine good looks.
- Is led through town by Dionysus dressed like a woman.
- Spies on the Maenads from the top of a tree.
- Is ripped apart by Agave and the other Maenads.

Chorus Character Analysis

Euripides has often been criticized for his use of choruses, mainly because they rarely affect the action of the play. This is definitely true of the Chorus in *The Bacchae*, which is pretty interesting because the play is named after them. These ladies have followed Dionysus all the way from Asia to help spread his religion, but end up doing very little to help out. OK, they do make an attempt once in a while. For example, when King Pentheus shows up talking lots of junk about Dionysus, the Chorus tells him he'd better stop with the blasphemy or he'll be in trouble. Of course, Pentheus just ignores them. You can't blame the Chorus too much though; the King doesn't listen to anybody else either.

The Chorus seems to spend most of to time singing praises to their god, Dionysus. These hymns don't affect the plot, but they do give the play a sense of ritual. Here's a typical passage:

My love is in the mountains
Limp upon the ground he
Sinks. The revel races,
Vested in his fawn skin, he
Hunts the goat and kill it…
Ecstasy the raw
Flesh…And to mountains
Of Phrygia, of Lydia
He rushes. He is Bromius [Dionysus]. (5)

Though the passage above in no way affects the plot of the play, it does help highlight the theme of man and the natural world. It also carries through the motif of hunting that is threaded throughout the play and gives a real sense of the wild ecstasy of Dionysus's rituals. It seems like Euripides just wasn't interested in using his choruses to further the plot of his plays and instead chose to use them for other purposes entirely. Euripides was a rebel in many ways. His unique use of choruses is just one of many examples of how he walked his own dramaturgical path. As he got older, choruses became less and less necessary to the plots of his plays. Some scholars theorize that if he'd had his way, he would gotten rid of them all together. This drastic step would have been sacrilege in the Athenian dramatic competitions, though.

Chorus Timeline and Summary

- Sings a song in praise of Dionysus.
- Gives a little back-story on Dionysus's birth.
- Praises Dionysus some more.
- Chastises Pentheus for being blasphemous.
- Sings about the dangers of blasphemy.
- Does some praising.
- Curses Pentheus for locking up their leader (really Dionysus).

- Begs their god to help them.
- Sings about nature.
- Warns against blasphemy again.
- Prays for Pentheus's punishment.
- Celebrates the King's grisly death.
- Praises (you guessed it) Dionysus.
- Warns against defying the gods.

Character Roles

Protagonist
Dionysus
There's no doubt that Dionysus is the protagonist of *The Bacchae*. He's the center around which the play revolves. He's the one who disturbs the world of the play by bringing his new religion home to Thebes. Most importantly, Dionysus is the one who drives the action of the play. He shows up at the beginning, tells us he's going to punish all the foolish mortals who are defying him, and that's just what he does. Dionysus is a great example of a truly active protagonist.

Though Dionysus is the protagonist, it may be kind of hard to think of him as a "good guy." A lot of people try to pigeonhole the role of protagonist in this way, but very often it just doesn't apply. Dionysus does a lot of messed up stuff during the play and all for his personal pride. Though there is a hey-lets-frolic-in-the-woods side to him, there's also a hey-lets-rip-people-apart side. Such un-heroic heroes are pretty typical of Euripides. Check out our guide to *Medea* if you're looking for another example.

Antagonist
Pentheus
King Pentheus bears all the hallmarks of an antagonist. The easiest way to figure out who fills this role is to first ask yourself, "What does the protagonist want?" Then ask, "Who's standing the way of that thing?" It's pretty clear that Pentheus is the force that Dionysus is up against. He's the guy standing in the way of the god's attempt to spread his new religion.

We'd also just like to point out that as antagonists go Pentheus is pretty weak. He's got nothing on, say, Lord Voldemort or Darth Vader. Ultimately he's just not a particularly tough adversary for Dionysus. We're not trying to diss on him or anything, he's just made the unfortunate decision to antagonize a god. There's just not a whole lot a mortal can do in the face of divine power.

Also, though Pentheus is kind of jerk sometimes he's not much of a "bad guy." Sure he's bullheaded and he's got a temper, but ultimately he's just trying to keep his city from falling into chaos. Pentheus is just trying to be a good king. Pentheus is a great example of how not all antagonists necessarily have to be ill intentioned.

Foil

Dionysus to Pentheus

Dionysus and Pentheus are classic example of foils. Dionysus is a wild god of nature. Pentheus is a law-abiding mortal of the city. Dionysus favors crazy revelry. Pentheus is into law and order. Dionysus represents unbridled primal energy. Pentheus represents the world of reason. The two characters really couldn't be more different.

The contrast between these two characters becomes symbolic of a conflict that perhaps exists within all human beings: the rational vs. the irrational. The idea is that we've all got a little crazy bubbling underneath the surface, a Dionysian world of pure instinct and emotion that our logical Pentheian side struggles to control. Maybe within us all there's a Dionysus and Pentheus at war.

Character Clues

Type of Being

The huge gap between being a god and being a mortal is felt pretty keenly in *The Bacchae*. The god, Dionysus, makes mince meat of all the puny humans who oppose him. Pentheus, Agave, and all the rest of Thebes are all helpless in the face his holy wrath. The god's unchecked unstoppable power is essential in defining his character. The inability of the human characters to do anything to stop him highlights not only their own helplessness, but also the helplessness of all human beings in the face of nature.

Actions

The word "drama" comes from the Greek word for action. Given that, it's probably no surprise that most characters in most dramas are defined by their actions. *The Bacchae* is no exception to this. For example Dionysus's complex character is shown through the things he does. The god is capable of inspiring beautiful harmony with nature as well as horrible violence. King Pentheus's actions also show just what kind of guy he is. He spends the whole play, trying to squelch Dionysus's wild rituals. This action seems to show the King's dedication to law and order, and reveals his stiffly logical mind.

Speech and Dialogue

Dialogue is pretty much the only tool a playwright has available to create character. Well, there are stage directions, but ancient Greek playwrights never wrote them down. (Note: If there are stage directions in the version you read they were probably put there by the translator or editor.) In any case, you can definitely get a sense of who the characters in *The Bacchae* are by the way they speak.

Some good scenes to look to for examples of characterization through speech are the ones between Dionysus and Pentheus. The god speaks mostly in riddles and elusive statements. This not only shows his skill with language, but also highlights his wily nature. Pentheus, on the other hand, is no match for the god's verbal gymnastics. He mostly responds to the god in direct, surface-level questions. This difference in the way the two characters speak directly reflects the contrast between the two characters.

Literary Devices

Symbols, Imagery, Allegory

The City vs. the Wild
Euripides contrasts images of the natural world with the world of man throughout *The Bacchae*. All through the text, the playwright compares the walled city of Thebes with the wild landscapes that surround it. These two differing locations seem to be symbolic of the central conflict of the play. On the one side we have nature, which could represent untamed irrationality. On the other side we have the human-built city of Thebes, which could be seen as symbolic of ordered rationality.

We should also note that both Dionysus and Pentheus become symbolic of the environment they prefer. The god calls his followers out into the woods and mountains to engage in his wild rituals, while the King struggles to maintain order behind the walls of his solid stone city. Some scholars say that one of the main points of *The Bacchae* is to show the danger of man attempting to totally suppress natural forces. When Pentheus tries to imprison Dionysus, nature goes berserk. Lightning and earthquakes shake and ravage the King's carefully ordered city.

Man and Nature in Harmony
Nature isn't only depicted as a force of destruction in *The Bacchae*. Euripides also gives a quite a bit of imagery which could be seen as symbolic of the possible harmony between man and the wild. The Herdsman's report to King Pentheus is full of these kinds of images. He tells the King that "Some [Maenads] fondled young gazelles or untamed wolf cubs in their arms and fed them with their own milk" (119). This image of the women nurturing young animals seems to be symbolic of the possible union between humans and nature. The Herdsman goes on to say that, "Anyone who fancied liquid white to drink just scratched the soil with fingertips and got herself a jet of milk" (119). Here we see that the relationship can be reciprocal. Perhaps the point is that if we as human beings give to nature it will give back to us.

Animals
Animal imagery plays a big part in *The Bacchae*. For one, Euripides constantly summons the image of the fawn. Fawn skins were one of main pieces of attire for your average Bacchant. Early in the play we see Tiresias and Cadmus all decked out in their fawn skins as they go off to pay tribute to Dionysus. The fawn could be seen as symbolic of freedom and innocence. We hear the Chorus also express a longing to dance again like a "fawn at play in the green joy of a meadow," after it's escaped "the hallowing huntsman and his racing hounds" (171). This imagery also ties into the motif of hunting that's threaded throughout the play, and highlights the contrast of man and nature.

Another animal that pops up a lot in *The Bacchae* is the bull. One example is when the Herdsman and his buddies try to apprehend Agave and the other Maenads. This turns out to be a really bad idea, because the women go crazy and rip the men's cattle apart with their bare hands. The Herdsman laments that his "great lordly bulls" were "dragged to the ground like carcasses" (119). This kind of ritual dismemberment was often a part of Dionysian rituals, and is perhaps the reason that the bull became symbolic of the god. Dionysus even appears to the beguiled Pentheus as a bull before leading the King to be dismembered himself. Pentheus says, "Now I'd say your head was horned. […] for certainly you've changed – oh into a bull" (178). So, why would Dionysus choose to appear as an animal that he seemed to be a fan of dismembering? Your guess is as good as ours.

Setting

Thebes, Greece

The Bacchae is set in the ancient city-state of Thebes. It's interesting that though most Greek tragedians lived in Athens, their plays are hardly ever set there. In fact, it wasn't allowed. Maybe it just hit to close to home. Even so, the tragedies did almost always examine issues that Athens was currently wrestling with. Perhaps Athenians preferred a little objective distance when thinking about their problems.

Athenians also seemed to dig objective distance in terms of time. Tragedies were almost always set back in the day, somewhere in Greece's distant, mythical past. Euripides and his fellow tragedians drew from their culture's rich tradition of heroes and gods to weave their tales. The myth of Dionysus's punishment of the blasphemous Pentheus would have been well known to the ancient Athenian audience.

It's interesting that for the entire play we are within the walls of the city of Thebes. One of the central themes is man vs. nature or the city vs. the wild. At first we just hear about the wilderness outside the city through messenger speeches. Eventually, though, nature encroaches. Lightning, fire, and earthquakes ravage the Pentheus's well-ordered town as Dionysus makes the city his own.

Genre

Drama, Tragedy

We say the play is a drama because, umm…it's a play, a piece of literature that can only be fully appreciated when it's put in front of a live audience. More specifically we dub it a tragedy. Of course, Euripides the great rule breaker and genre bender, had his own ideas about tragedy – ideas that differed greatly from the concepts Aristotle would later pen in his *Poetics*.

For example, the protagonist of *The Bacchae*, the god Dionysus, has no *hamartia*, most often called a tragic flaw, but more accurately translated as a mistake in judgment. A hero or heroine's *hamartia* typically causes their undoing. This just isn't true with Dionysus.

Dionysus is a god, he can't do wrong, right? He sets out to punish the mortals who've denied him and gets just what he wants. Usually, a tragic hero suffers for his mistakes, but Dionysus emerges from the play triumphant. (You can read more about how *The Bacchae* doesn't fit the typical tragedy mold in "What's Up with the Ending?") We should note that that this isn't the first time this sort of thing happens in Euripides work. Just check out our guide to *Medea* for another example.

Tone

Comic, Tragic

The Bacchae is amazing in that for all tragic woe it presents, it's still got tons of laughs. Old Cadmus and Tiresias doing a clumsy jig, the beguiled King Pentheus prancing around in women's clothes – all this in a play with ritual dismemberment and a mother parading through town with her own son's head in her hand. The blending of comic and tragic is an amazing innovation by Euripides. He really was a true dramatic pioneer.

Writing Style

Modern

Euripides' style is often said to be much more "modern" than Aeschylus or Sophocles, the other great tragedians. This is because his dialogue often sounds almost conversational, much like modern realism. His characters speak in way that's a lot more like everyday speech than in most other Greek tragedies. This is definitely true in *The Bacchae*. Sure the play still uses heightened language and was composed in verse, but in comparison to his contemporaries, Euripides was a totally modern kind of guy.

What's Up With the Title?

Ancient Greek tragedians never got too creative with their titles. *The Bacchae* is named after the worshipers of Bacchus (a.k.a. Dionysus). These lovely ladies (check out our "Character Analysis" for the Bacchae) serve as the Chorus of the play, and support the protagonist, Dionysus, on his quest for punishment. We should note that sometimes translators dub the play *The Bacchants* or *The Bacchantes*, which are just other ways of saying *Bacchae*.

What's Up With the Ending?

The ending of *The Bacchae* is remarkable because nobody learns anything. If you listen to Aristotle, tragedies are supposed to end with the hero having an *anagnorisis*. This is Greek for a moment of realization or recognition. Basically, it's the part of the play where the hero goes, "Oh my gosh, I really messed up." According to Aristotle, the *anagnorisis* is supposed to happen to the play's protagonist. However, Dionysus, the protagonist of *The Bacchae*, isn't sorry one bit. He's happy as a bug in a rug about the horror he's caused. Making all the ladies of Thebes go crazy and dismember cattle? Awesome. Causing Agave to rip her son Pentheus's head off? A job well done. Dionysus set out to show everybody who's boss and that's just what he's done. At the end of the play, he's completely unrepentant.

You do see a bit of an *anagnorisis* with Agave. She definitely has a moment of recognition, when she realizes that the bloody head she's holding is actually her son's and not a lion's. She's definitely sorry for doing it. The thing is it doesn't really count because Dionysus is the one that took over her mind and made her do it. Agave isn't sorry at all for spurning Dionysus to begin with. When Dionysus tells her she's banished she complains the god is "merciless" (313). As she exits the stage, she's not thinking, "Well, next time I'm going to mind my manners when a new god comes around." Instead she says, "Let others meddle with Bacchants" (332). Agave doesn't seem to be sorry at all, she's just mad the whole thing happened.

The only person who says he's in the wrong at the end is Cadmus. The old man pleads with Dionysus saying, "Have mercy, Dionysus, we have sinned" (311). This is pretty ironic, because Cadmus was the only one in the family who willingly worshiped Dionysus. We think it's kind of weird that nobody mentions this here. Did everybody just forget the scene where Cadmus and Tiresias set off to dance in the mountains dressed up in fawn skins? Apparently, no one cares about that, least of all Dionysus, who dooms the old man to leading a barbarian horde in the form of a snake. So, let's get this straight – the only one who's sorry at the end of the play didn't really do anything wrong, but is punished anyway. What is the meaning of this, Euripides?

It's really no wonder that, in his *Poetics*, Aristotle talked a lot of smack about Euripides. These two guys obviously had different ideas of what a tragedy was supposed to be. The lack of any true *anagnorisis* in the conclusion of *The Bacchae* highlights their stark differences. Euripides's plays consistently present a cynical view of both man and the gods. But this attitude just didn't seem to compute with Aristotle's ideas of the universe. Euripides's tragedies are very rarely about the tragedy of one person who suffers and learns from that suffering. Instead Euripides often presents the tragedy of all humankind, being trapped in a harsh, chaotic, and unsympathetic universe.

Did You Know?

Trivia

- Euripides wrote *The Bacchae* while in Macedonia not Greece. (Source)
- The play was premiered in Athens after Euripides's death and was directed by his sons. (Source)
- Euripides saw the rise and fall of Athens as a major power during his lifetime. (Source)
- The philosopher Socrates had a big effect on the ideas in Euripides's plays. (Source)

Steaminess Rating

PG-13

There's plenty of talk of sex in *The Bacchae*. Pentheus imagines that his mother and the other Maenads are out in the mountains having wild orgies. However, everybody that goes out to observe the ladies, reports back that there is indeed no hanky-panky going on. These women seem to prefer ripping men apart with their bare hands rather than making love to them.

Allusions and Cultural References

Mythical References

- Zeus (1,4, 21, 22, 37, 38, 83, 94, 119, 170, 310)
- Hera (1, 22)
- Rhea (1, 4)
- Cybele (2)
- Fates (2)
- Aphrodite (21, 29)
- Demeter (22)
- Ares (22, 319)
- Apollo (22)
- Artemis (24)
- http://www.theoi.com/Ouranios/Erotes.html (29)
- Orpheus (84)
- Ennosis (89)

Best of the Web

Websites

Aristotle
http://www2.cnr.edu/home/bmcmanus/poetics.html
This page provides a good overview of Aristotle's thoughts on tragedy. Interestingly, Aristotle thought that Euripides's work didn't measure up.

Euripides's Biography
http://www.theatrehistory.com/ancient/euripides001.html

Click here for a great bio on Euripides.

Movie or TV Productions

The Bacchae
http://www.imdb.com/title/tt0154187/
Here's a 2002 movie version.

Backanterna
http://www.imdb.com/title/tt0313247/
This is a 1993 TV version directed by the famous Ingmar Bergman.

Historical Documents

Full Text
http://www.gutenberg.org/etext/15081
Here's a link to a collection of Euripides's tragedies, including   *The Bacchae*. It's not the translation we used, but it may be interesting to compare.

Aristotle's *Poetics*
http://classics.mit.edu/Aristotle/poetics.html
Read what Aristotle had to say about tragedy.

NY Times
http://theater2.nytimes.com/2008/07/05/theater/reviews/05bacc.html
A review of the National Theatre of Scotland's production.

The Bacchae at the Public.
http://www.newyorktheatreguide.com/news/may09/bacchae28may09.htm
An announcement the most recent NY production directed by Joann Akalaitis.

Video

National Theatre of Scotland
http://www.youtube.com/watch?v=LnHm3IPmpuU
Some clips from the National Theatre of Scotland's 2008 production.

The 5th Chorus
http://www.youtube.com/watch?v=2QbgJ22eTqQ
The fifth chorus of the play as staged for PBS.

The opening.
http://video.google.com/videoplay?docid=-4429558184398980677&ei=EKiqSoybNZ_sqAOW5L
SsAw&q=The+Bacchae+Euripides&hl=en#docid=1301070188832506470
Here's video of the opening scenes of the play.

Images

The Death of Pentheus
http://www.mlahanas.de/Greeks/Mythology/Images/PentheusBacchae.jpg
Here's a classic image of Pentheus's dismemberment at the hands of the Maenads.

Pentheus's Dismemberment on a Bowl
http://www.utexas.edu/courses/larrymyth/images/dionysus/GA-Pentheus-Douris.jpg
Looks like the Greeks had pretty morbid taste in dinnerware.

Alan Cumming
http://www.playbill.com/images/photo/b/a/bacchaeprod460.jpg
Here's an image of the famous actor Alan Cumming staring in *The Bacchae*.

Dionysus: Bull, Man, God
http://www.twistedtree.org.uk/dionysus_as_bull.jpg
Here's an image showing Dionysus in his bovine form.

Printed in Great Britain
by Amazon

38995316R00032